Other books by Mick Inkpen:

KIPPER
KIPPER'S TOYBOX
KIPPER'S BIRTHDAY
KIPPER'S BOOK OF COLOURS
KIPPER'S BOOK OF OPPOSITES
KIPPER'S BOOK OF WEATHER
ONE BEAR AT BEDTIME
THE BLUE BALLOON
THREADBEAR
BILLY'S BEETLE
PENGUIN SMALL
LULLABYHULLABALLOO!
WIBBLY PIG BOARD BOOKS
NOTHING

British Library Cataloguing in Publication Data

A catalogue record for this book is available
from the British Library

ISBN 0 340 63481 2

First published 1994
First paperback edition 1996
10 9 8 7 6 5 4 3 2

Published by Hodder Children's Books,
a division of Hodder Headline plc,
338 Euston Road, London NW1 3BH

Printed in Italy by L.E.G.O., Vicenza

KIPPER'S BOOK OF
COUNTING
Mick Inkpen

*Hodder
Children's
Books*

a division of Hodder Headline plc

1

One Kipper

2
Two hedgehogs

3

Three hamsters

4

Four hens

5

Five tortoises

6
Six moles

7
Seven chicks

8

Eight frogs

9

Nine snails

10
And ten friends!